AF269859

GREATEST OF ALL TIME PLAYERS

G.O.A.T. FOOTBALL SAFETIES

Audrey Stewart

Lerner Publications ◆ Minneapolis

Lerner Publications Company
An imprint of Lerner Publishing Group, Inc.
241 First Avenue North
Minneapolis, MN 55401 USA

For reading levels and more information, look up this title at www.lernerbooks.com.

Main body text set in Aptifer Sans LT Pro.
Typeface provided by Linotype AG.

Library of Congress Cataloging-in-Publication Data

Names: Stewart, Audrey, author.
Title: G.O.A.T. football safeties / Audrey Stewart.
Other titles: Greatest of all time football safeties
Description: Minneapolis, MN : Lerner Publications , [2025] | Series: Greatest of all time players | Includes bibliographical references and index. | Audience: Ages 7–11 | Audience: Grades 2–3 | Summary: "Football safeties do it all. They defend against passes, make big hits on running backs, and sack the quarterback. But who are the greatest safeties in NFL history? Meet the players and make your picks!"—Provided by publisher.
Identifiers: LCCN 2023049845 (print) | LCCN 2023049846 (ebook) | ISBN 9798765625859 (library binding) | ISBN 9798765628812 (paperback) | ISBN 9798765633922 (epub)
Subjects: LCSH: Defensive backs (Football)—United States—Biography—Juvenile literature. | Football players—United States—Biography—Juvenile literature.
Classification: LCC GV939.A1 S75 2025 (print) | LCC GV939.A1 (ebook) | DDC 796.332092/2—dc23/eng/20231026

LC record available at https://lccn.loc.gov/2023049845
LC ebook record available at https://lccn.loc.gov/2023049846

Manufactured in the United States of America
1 – CG – 7/15/24

TABLE OF CONTENTS

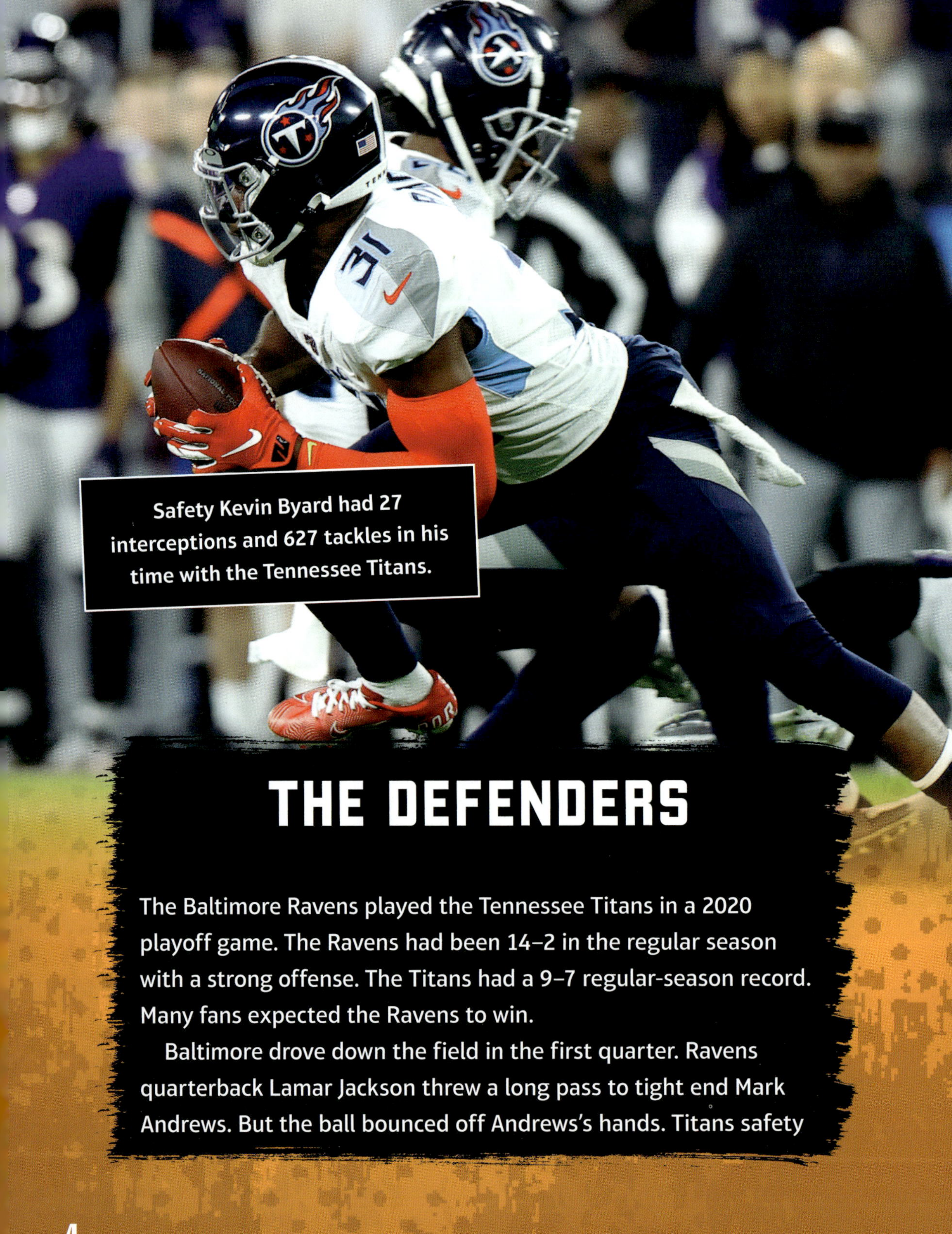

THE DEFENDERS

The Baltimore Ravens played the Tennessee Titans in a 2020 playoff game. The Ravens had been 14–2 in the regular season with a strong offense. The Titans had a 9–7 regular-season record. Many fans expected the Ravens to win.

Baltimore drove down the field in the first quarter. Ravens quarterback Lamar Jackson threw a long pass to tight end Mark Andrews. But the ball bounced off Andrews's hands. Titans safety

FACTS AT A GLANCE

» **EMLEN TUNNELL** WAS THE FIRST BLACK PLAYER TO JOIN THE NEW YORK GIANTS AND THE PRO FOOTBALL HALL OF FAME.

» **PAUL KRAUSE** HOLDS THE NATIONAL FOOTBALL LEAGUE (NFL) RECORD FOR MOST INTERCEPTIONS OF ALL TIME WITH 81. TWELVE OF THEM WERE DURING HIS FIRST SEASON.

» **ED REED** SET A RECORD FOR THE LONGEST INTERCEPTION RETURN IN NFL HISTORY. HE INTERCEPTED A PASS AND RETURNED IT 107 YARDS FOR A TOUCHDOWN.

» **WILLIE WOOD** PLAYED IN THE FIRST SUPER BOWL IN 1967 BETWEEN THE GREEN BAY PACKERS AND THE KANSAS CITY CHIEFS.

Kevin Byard caught the ball for an interception and ran 31 yards before going out of bounds. The Titans took over and scored a touchdown for an early lead.

Byard's big play helped the Titans beat the Ravens 28–12. He led the Titans defense with one interception and 11 tackles. Tennessee advanced to the American Football Conference (AFC) Championship game.

Kevin Byard (*top*)

Safeties are defensive backs. They usually start each play far away from the line of scrimmage. But their role can shift based on the play. If the team runs a blitz, safeties might start closer to the line to attack the quarterback.

Ed Reed spent most of his NFL career as a safety for the Baltimore Ravens.

On other plays, safeties run with wide receivers to defend against passes. Safeties also tackle running backs on running plays. Before a play starts, the opposing quarterback might look to see where the safeties are to find a weak spot in the defense. The best safeties cover their teams' weak spots and make it very hard for the other team to score.

ERIC BERRY

The Kansas City Chiefs picked Eric Berry in the first round of the 2010 NFL Draft. He started at safety in all 16 games and was a Pro Bowl player in his rookie season. He played back-to-back Pro Bowl games in 2012 and 2013 and was a First-Team All-Pro player in 2013. That year, he had three interceptions, two touchdowns, two forced fumbles, and 74 tackles.

Berry missed part of the 2014 season because of an ankle injury. He returned to action but left the team in late November to receive treatment for cancer. In 2015, he won the NFL Comeback Player of the Year award. He had 61 tackles, two interceptions, and 10 passes defended that season. Berry was a force for the Chiefs defense as the team went on an 11-game winning streak.

Each season, the NFL releases its Top 100 Players list. Berry made it onto the list in 2016 and 2017. He made a big impact in his nine NFL seasons.

ERIC BERRY STATS

	Career Touchdowns	5
	First-Team All-Pro	3 Times
	Career Interceptions	14
	Longest Interception Return	54 Yards

WILLIE WOOD

Willie Wood didn't join the Green Bay Packers through the NFL Draft like most players did. He asked the team for a tryout and a chance to prove himself. And he did just that. Wood joined the Packers in 1960 and became a top safety in the league. He won First- or Second-Team All-NFL honors nine times in his 12-year career. Wood played in the Pro Bowl in 1963, and then back-to-back Pro Bowls from 1965 to 1971. He helped the Packers become NFL champions five times.

Wood was the starting safety for Green Bay in the first and second Super Bowls in 1967 and 1968. In the 1967 Super Bowl against the Chiefs, Wood returned an interception 50 yards to set up a touchdown. It was Wood's longest interception return ever in a playoff game, and the Packers won 35–10. Wood is one of Green Bay's greatest players of all time. He retired from playing in 1972.

WILLIE WOOD STATS

🏈	Career Touchdowns	4
🏈	Pro Bowls	8
🏈	Career Interceptions	48
🏈	Longest Interception Return	42 Yards

TROY POLAMALU

Troy Polamalu was a top player for the Pittsburgh Steelers from 2003 to 2015. In 2004, he began playing safety. His teammates nicknamed him the Tasmanian Devil for his high-energy style of play. Polamalu played in the Pro Bowl five straight seasons from 2005 to 2009.

In the second game of the 2010 season, Polamalu thrilled Steelers fans and helped his team beat the Tennessee Titans. The Titans were about to score. But Polamalu leaped over the line of scrimmage to sack Titans quarterback Kerry Collins. Polamalu shut down the play, and the Steelers won 19–11. From 2011 to 2014, Polamalu was on the NFL Top 100 Players list. He retired from playing after the 2014 season with 12 career sacks and 783 tackles. Polamalu joined the Pro Football Hall of Fame in 2020.

TROY POLAMALU STATS

 Career Touchdowns — 5

 First-Team All-Pro — 4 Times

 Career Interceptions — 32

 Longest Interception Return — 49 Yards

JACK CHRISTIANSEN

Jack Christiansen was a football and track All-American athlete at Colorado State University. Christiansen was 6 feet 1 (1.9 m) and 162 pounds (73.5 kg), and some people thought he was too small to play in the NFL. But he joined the Detroit Lions in 1951 and proved them wrong. Christiansen scored four times in two games on punt returns.

Christiansen was great on returns, but he was even better at safety. He and the Lions dominated in the 1950s. They won four division titles and NFL championships in 1952, 1953, and 1957. Christiansen played during some of Detroit's best years. He was such a great leader that people called Detroit's defense Chris's Crew in his honor. Christiansen led the league in interceptions for the 1953 and 1957 seasons. He played in his final Pro Bowl in 1958 and retired after the next season.

JACK CHRISTIANSEN STATS

 Career Touchdowns — 13

 Pro Bowls — 5

 Career Interceptions — 46

 Longest Interception Return — 92 Yards

KEVIN BYARD

The Tennessee Titans picked Kevin Byard in the 2016 NFL Draft. He was a Pro Bowler in just his second season. Byard recorded eight interceptions in 2017 and tied for first in the NFL. For the 2018 and 2019 seasons, Byard started every game and caught nine total interceptions. He had a career-high 111 tackles for the 2020 season.

Byard's success comes from his ability to track the opposing quarterback. He can predict where the quarterback will throw the ball. This skill has also helped him earn four career sacks. Byard is strong and fast.

During the 2021 season, the Titans played the Jacksonville Jaguars. The game started with a Jaguars fumble. Byard got the ball and sprinted to the end zone for his first career touchdown. The Titans won 37–19. Byard finished the game with one interception and 11 tackles and earned the AFC Defensive Player of the Month award for October. Byard joined the Philadelphia Eagles in 2023.

KEVIN BYARD STATS

	Career Touchdowns	2
	Pro Bowls	2
	Career Interceptions	28
	Longest Interception Return	33 Yards

Stats are accurate through the 2023 NFL season.

ED REED

Ed Reed was a master at intercepting the ball. The Baltimore Ravens picked Reed in the first round of the 2002 NFL Draft. He played 11 seasons with the team. In his first season, Reed started all 16 games. He had 85 tackles, five interceptions, one sack, and one fumble recovery. Reed led the Ravens in interceptions in seven of his 11 seasons with the team.

Reed's interception during the 2013 Super Bowl is one of his best moments. San Francisco 49ers quarterback Colin Kaepernick threw to wide receiver Randy Moss, but the ball was too high for Moss. Reed grabbed it. He tied an NFL record with nine career interceptions in the playoffs with this catch. The Ravens won 34–31, marking Reed's only Super Bowl championship. He holds the NFL record for most career interception return yards with 1,590. He also has the two longest interception returns at 106 and 107 yards.

ED REED STATS

	Career Touchdowns	13
	Pro Bowls	9
	Career Interceptions	64
	Longest Interception Return	107 Yards

DERWIN JAMES JR.

The Los Angeles Chargers picked Derwin James Jr. in the 2018 NFL Draft. He played in the 2018 Pro Bowl and earned a First-Team All-Pro spot. James started all 16 games with the Chargers that season. He had three interceptions and defended 13 passes. He also had 105 tackles.

The 2022 season was a great one for James. In a game against the Kansas City Chiefs, he tracked a pass to tight end Travis Kelce. Kelce caught the ball, but James tossed him to the ground before he could score. James won the AFC Defensive Player of the Month award for November 2022. He finished the 2022 season with 115 tackles, four sacks, two forced fumbles, and two interceptions.

James led the Chargers defense again in 2023, logging 125 tackles in the regular season. His 86 solo tackles were the 10th highest in the league. James was part of the NFL's Top 100 Players of 2023.

DERWIN JAMES JR. STATS

 Career Sacks — 11.5

 Pro Bowls — 3

 Career Interceptions — 8

 Longest Interception Return — 23 Yards

Stats are accurate through the 2023 NFL season.

PAUL KRAUSE

Paul Krause is the NFL's all-time interceptions leader. He started out playing both baseball and football at the University of Iowa. A shoulder injury made him decide to focus only on football.

The Washington Redskins picked Krause in the second round of the 1964 NFL Draft. He had an amazing rookie season. Krause led the NFL with 12 interceptions. He earned a spot on the First-Team All-Pro list and played in his first

Pro Bowl. Krause played four seasons and intercepted 28 passes for Washington. He moved to the Minnesota Vikings in 1968.

In his first season with the Vikings, Krause had interceptions in six straight games. In 1975, he logged a Vikings team best with 10 interceptions for the season. Krause still holds the team record. He broke an NFL record in 1979 with 81 career pass interceptions.

Krause never won a championship. But he made four Super Bowl appearances as the Vikings starting safety in 1970, 1974, 1975, and 1977. Krause joined the Pro Football Hall of Fame in 1998.

PAUL KRAUSE STATS

🏈	Career Touchdowns	6
🏈	Pro Bowls	8
🏈	Career Interceptions	81
🏈	Longest Interception Return	81 Yards

NO. 2 MINKAH FITZPATRICK

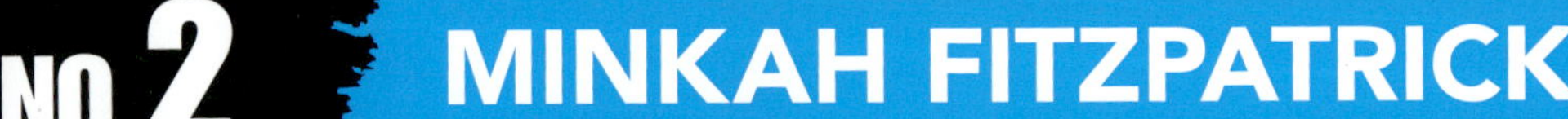

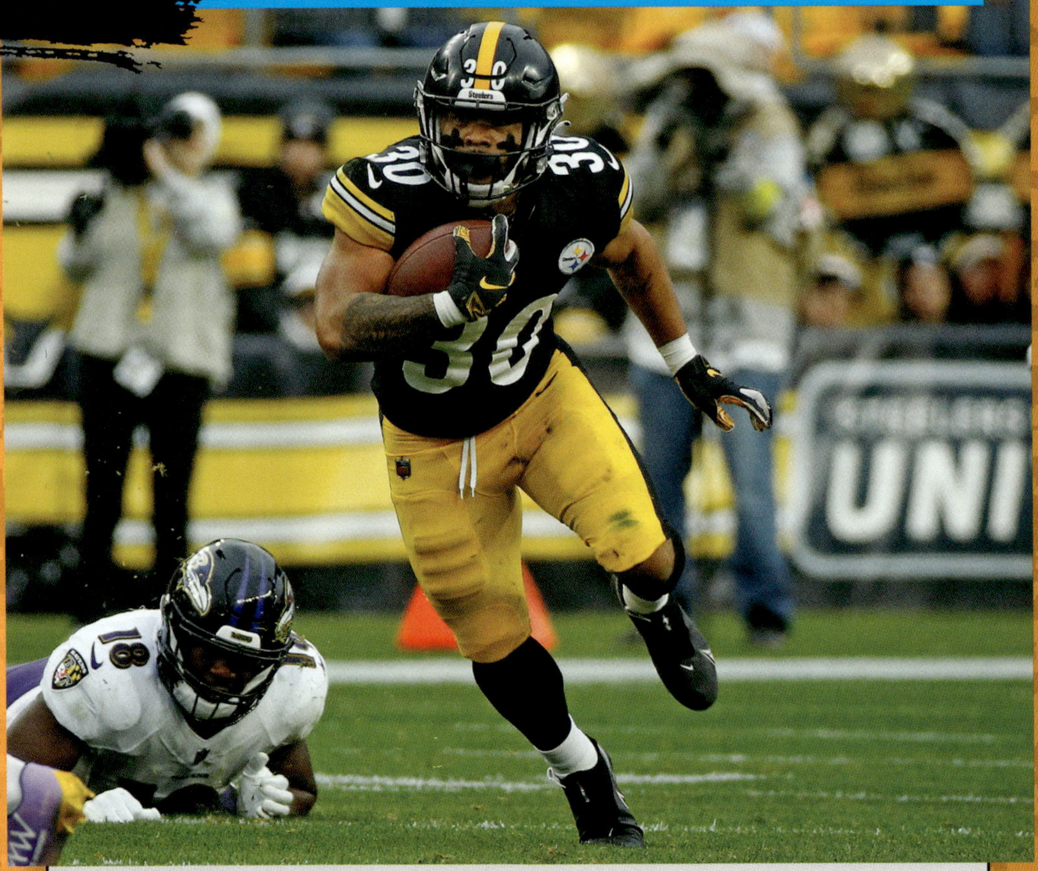

Minkah Fitzpatrick is strong and fast. His career started with the Miami Dolphins in 2018. He joined the Pittsburgh Steelers for most of the 2019 season. As a second-year player, Fitzpatrick had a 96-yard return for a touchdown and seven tackles in a game against the Indianapolis Colts. He finished the season with two touchdowns, 69 tackles, and five interceptions.

In a 2022 matchup against the Cincinnati Bengals, Fitzpatrick started work early. He stepped in front of a pass intended for wide receiver Tyler Bowl and intercepted it. Fitzpatrick returned it 31 yards for a touchdown.

At halftime, the Steelers led 17–6. But the Bengals came back and tied the game 20–20 in the fourth quarter. With two seconds on the game clock, Cincinnati was a moment away from winning. The extra point after a touchdown would have sealed the game for the Bengals. But Fitzpatrick blocked the ball. The Steelers won 23–20 in overtime. Fitzpatrick is a three-time Pro Bowl player.

MINKAH FITZPATRICK STATS

 Career Touchdowns — 5

 Pro Bowls — 4

 Career Interceptions — 19

 Longest Interception Return — 96 Yards

Stats are accurate through the 2023 NFL season.

EMLEN TUNNELL

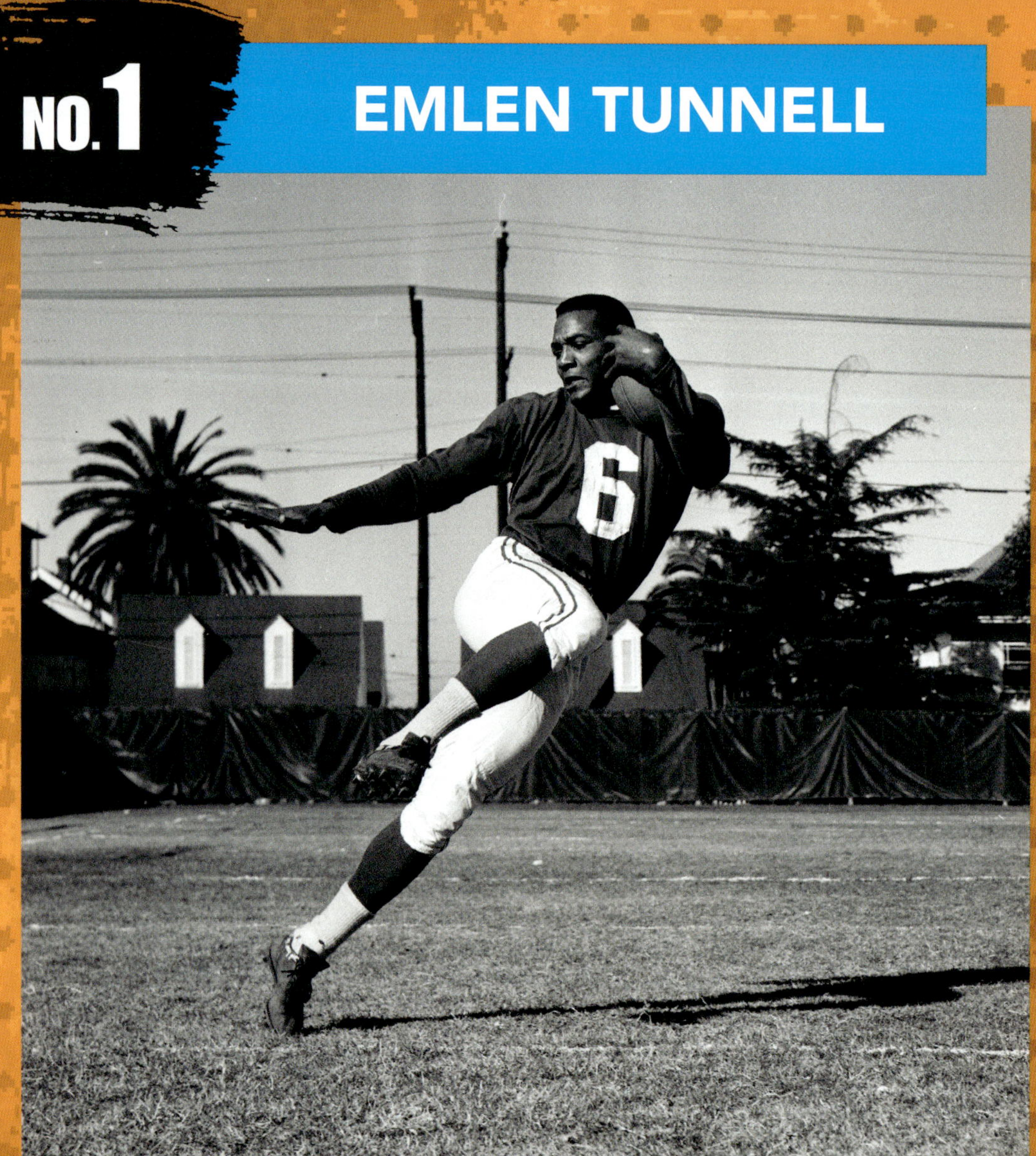

Emlen Tunnell had a unique path to pro football. Tunnell wanted to play for the New York Giants. In 1948, he traveled to New York City and asked team founder Tim Mara for a tryout. The Giants agreed, and he became the first Black player to play for the team.

Tunnell was a top safety from 1949 to 1953. In 1950, he ranked second in the NFL with 305 punt return yards. He was fourth in the NFL with 167 interception return yards.

The following year was Tunnell's best. During the 1951 season, he led the NFL with a career-high 489 punt return yards. In 1952, he gained 923 yards on interceptions and kickoff returns. That was more than the NFL rushing leader earned that year. In 1959, Tunnell followed coach Vince Lombardi to the Green Bay Packers. Tunnell retired from playing in 1961 after three seasons with the Packers. He joined the Pro Football Hall of Fame in 1967.

EMLEN TUNNELL STATS

Career Touchdowns	10
Pro Bowls	9
Career Interceptions	79
Longest Interception Return	55 Yards

EVEN MORE G.O.A.T.

There have been so many amazing safeties in NFL history. Choosing only 10 is a challenge. Here are 10 others who could have made the G.O.A.T. list.

No. 11	RONNIE LOTT
No. 12	YALE LARY
No. 13	MICAH HYDE
No. 14	KENNY EASLEY
No. 15	ADRIAN AMOS
No. 16	STEVE ATWATER
No. 17	DEVIN MCCOURTY
No. 18	JOHNNY ROBINSON
No. 19	DICK ANDERSON
No. 20	CHARLIE WATERS

YOUR G.O.A.T.

It's your turn to make a G.O.A.T. list about football safeties. Start by doing research. Consider the rankings in this book. Then check out the Learn More section on page 31. Explore the books and websites to learn more about football players of the past and present.

You can search online for more information about great players too. Check with a librarian, who may have other resources for you. You might even try reaching out to football teams or players to see what they think.

Once you're ready, make your list of the greatest players of all time. Then ask people you know to make G.O.A.T. lists and compare them. Do you have players no one else listed? Are you missing anybody your friends think is important? Talk it over and try to convince them that your list is the G.O.A.T.!

GLOSSARY

blitz: when many defenders rush the quarterback at once

draft: when teams take turns choosing new players

First-Team All-Pro: a team made up of each season's best NFL players

fumble: when a football player loses hold of the ball while handling or running with it

interception: a pass caught by the defending team

line of scrimmage: an imaginary line where each play begins

Pro Bowl: the NFL's all-star game

punt: when a football player drops the ball and kicks it before it touches the ground

return: when a player runs with the ball after a kickoff, punt, fumble, or interception

rookie: a first-year player

sack: to tackle the quarterback behind the line of scrimmage

LEARN MORE

Anastasio, Dina. *What Is the Super Bowl?* New York: Penguin Young Readers Group, 2015.

Flynn, Brendan. *The Genius Kid's Guide to Pro Football.* Mendota Heights, MN: North Star Editions, 2022.

Football Defensive Back
https://www.rookieroad.com/football/positions/defensive-back/

Hill, Christina. *Inside the Pittsburgh Steelers.* Minneapolis: Lerner Publications, 2023.

Sports Illustrated Kids—Football
https://www.sikids.com/football

What Is a Safety in Football?
https://footballadvantage.com/safety-football/

INDEX

PHOTO ACKNOWLEDGMENTS

Image credits: Rob Carr/Staff/Getty Images, p.4; Todd Olszewski/Stringer/ Getty Images, p.5; Icon Sportswire/Contributor//Getty Images, p.6; Jason Miller/ Stringer/Getty Images, p.7; Scott Halleran/Staff/Getty Images, p.8; Peter G. Aiken/ Contributor/Getty Images, p.9; Focus On Sport/Contributor/Getty Images, p.10; Bettmann/Contributor/Getty Images, p.11; Ezra Shaw/Staff/Getty Images, p.12; Kirk Irwin/Contributor/Getty Images, p.13; Tim Culek/Contributor/Getty Images, p.14; The Enthusiast Network/Contributor/Getty Images, p.15; Kevin Sabitus/ Contributor/Getty Images, p.16; Cooper Neill/Contributor/Getty Images, p.17; Tom Hauck/Contributor/Getty Images, p.18; Al Pereira/Contributor/Getty Images, p.19; Perry Knotts/Contributor/Getty Images, p.20; Robert Gauthier/Contributor/ Getty Images, p.21; Clifton Boutelle/Contributor/Getty Images, p.22; Star Tribune via Getty Images/Contributor/Getty Images, p.23; Justin K. Aller/Contributor/ Getty Images, p.24; Justin Casterline/Contributor/Getty Images, p.25; University of Southern California/Contributor/Getty Images, p.26; Robert Riger/Contributor/ Getty Images, p.27

Cover: Tom Hauck/Contributor/Getty Images; Katelyn Mulcahy/Contributor/Getty Images; Justin K. Aller/Contributor/Getty Images